Published by Angelis Publications
ISBN: 978-1-912484-01-0
www.angelispublications.com
© Angelis Publications 2017

A Celebration of the Life of

_____

_____

_____

_____

_____

_____

When someone you love

becomes a memory,

the memory becomes

a treasure

Name & Address

Thoughts & Memories

Name & Address

Thoughts & Memories

Name & Address

_____

_____

_____

_____

_____

_____

_____

_____

_____

_____

_____

_____

_____

_____

Thoughts & Memories

_____

_____

_____

_____

_____

_____

_____

_____

_____

_____

_____

_____

_____

_____

Name & Address

Thoughts & Memories

Name & Address

Thoughts & Memories

Name & Address

Thoughts & Memories

Name & Address

Thoughts & Memories

Name & Address

Thoughts & Memories

Name & Address

Thoughts & Memories

Name & Address

Thoughts & Memories

Name & Address

Thoughts & Memories

Name & Address

Thoughts & Memories

Name & Address

Thoughts & Memories

Name & Address

Thoughts & Memories

Name & Address

Thoughts & Memories

Name & Address

_____

_____

_____

_____

_____

_____

_____

_____

_____

_____

_____

_____

Thoughts & Memories

_____

_____

_____

_____

_____

_____

_____

_____

_____

_____

Name & Address

Thoughts & Memories

Name & Address

Thoughts & Memories

Name & Address

Thoughts & Memories

Name & Address

Thoughts & Memories

Name & Address

Thoughts & Memories

Name & Address

Thoughts & Memories

Name & Address

Thoughts & Memories

Name & Address

Thoughts & Memories

Name & Address

Thoughts & Memories

Name & Address

Thoughts & Memories

Name & Address

Thoughts & Memories

Name & Address

Thoughts & Memories

Name & Address

Thoughts & Memories

Name & Address

Thoughts & Memories

Name & Address

Thoughts & Memories

Name & Address

Thoughts & Memories

Name & Address

Thoughts & Memories

Name & Address

Thoughts & Memories

Name & Address

Thoughts & Memories

Name & Address

Thoughts & Memories

Name & Address

Thoughts & Memories

Name & Address

Thoughts & Memories

Name & Address

Thoughts & Memories

Name & Address

Thoughts & Memories

Name & Address

Thoughts & Memories

Name & Address

Thoughts & Memories

Name & Address

Thoughts & Memories

Name & Address.

Thoughts & Memories

Name & Address

Thoughts & Memories

Name & Address

Thoughts & Memories

Name & Address

Thoughts & Memories

Name & Address

Thoughts & Memories

Name & Address

Thoughts & Memories

Name & Address

Thoughts & Memories

Name & Address

Thoughts & Memories

Name & Address

Thoughts & Memories

Name & Address

Thoughts & Memories

Name & Address

Thoughts & Memories

Name & Address

Thoughts & Memories

Name & Address

Thoughts & Memories

Name & Address

Thoughts & Memories

Name & Address

Thoughts & Memories

Name & Address

_____

_____

_____

_____

_____

_____

_____

_____

_____

_____

_____

_____

_____

Thoughts & Memories

_____

_____

_____

_____

_____

_____

_____

_____

_____

_____

_____

_____

_____

Name & Address

Thoughts & Memories

Name & Address

Thoughts & Memories

Name & Address

Thoughts & Memories

Name & Address

Thoughts & Memories

Name & Address

Thoughts & Memories

Name & Address

Thoughts & Memories

Name & Address

Thoughts & Memories

Name & Address

Thoughts & Memories

Name & Address

Thoughts & Memories

Name & Address

Thoughts & Memories

Name & Address

Thoughts & Memories

Name & Address

Thoughts & Memories

Name & Address

Thoughts & Memories

Name & Address

Thoughts & Memories

Name & Address

Thoughts & Memories

Name & Address

Thoughts & Memories

Name & Address

Thoughts & Memories

Name & Address

Thoughts & Memories

Name & Address

Thoughts & Memories

Name & Address

Thoughts & Memories

Name & Address

Thoughts & Memories

Name & Address

Thoughts & Memories

Name & Address

Thoughts & Memories

Name & Address

Thoughts & Memories

Name & Address

Thoughts & Memories

Name & Address

Thoughts & Memories

Name & Address

Thoughts & Memories

Name & Address

Thoughts & Memories

Name & Address

Thoughts & Memories

Name & Address

Thoughts & Memories

Name & Address

Thoughts & Memories

Name & Address

Thoughts & Memories

Name & Address

Thoughts & Memories

Name & Address

_____

_____

_____

_____

_____

_____

_____

_____

_____

_____

_____

_____

_____

Thoughts & Memories

_____

_____

_____

_____

_____

_____

_____

_____

_____

_____

_____

_____

_____

Name & Address

Thoughts & Memories

CPSIA information can be obtained
at www.ICGtesting.com
Printed in the USA
LVHW061659110621
689903LV00010B/969